Grass Whistle
AMY DRYANSKY

salmonpoetry

Published in 2013 by

Salmon Poetry

Cliffs of Moher, County Clare, Ireland

Website: www.salmonpoetry.com

Email: info@salmonpoetry.com

ISBN 978-1-908836-41-0

8/14

COVER ARTWORK: *Barbara Reid, www.barbarareid.org*
COVER DESIGN: *Siobhán Hutson*

Printed in Ireland by Sprint Print

For my family—past, present, future…

Acknowledgements

First and foremost, thanks to Jessie Lendennie and Salmon Poetry's unswerving commitment to poetry and poets, even in these austere times. Thanks also to the Five College Women's Studies Research Center at Mt. Holyoke College, where I found my context and this book was born. As always, deep gratitude to my family for their love and support, and to my friends, who keep me afloat in all kinds of rough weather. Special thanks to the brilliant and generous first readers and listeners of almost all of these poems: Elissa Alford, Markie Babbot, Annie Boutelle, Diana Gordon, Maya Janson, Mary Koncel, Carol Potter, Elizabeth Slade, Kristen Stake and Ellen Dore Watson.

Some of the poems in *Grass Whistle* appear in the following print and on-line publications:

Dogs Singing: A Tribute Anthology: "Happy As I Believe Myself to Be"
Harvard Review: "Point of Origin" (published as Biography)
make/shift: "Her Vital Statistics"
Morning Song (anthology, St. Martin's Press): "In the Tree House,"
    "Of All She Surveys"
Negative Capability: "Bow Season"
New England Watershed: "Somewhere Honey from those Bees"
    (This poem was also a finalist for the Poetry Society of America's
    Lucille Medwick Memorial Award).
Orion: "Because We've Landed on the Moon but Nobody Wants to
    Live There"
Poets for Living Waters: "Somewhere Honey from those Bees,"
    "Past A Certain Point of Magnification," "All Portraits
    Become Landscapes," "Because We've Landed on the Moon
    but Nobody Wants to Live There"
Post Road: "The Bed Was Made"
Salamander: "Dear Tender Place, Cake & Eat It, Too"
Myrrh, Mothwing, Smoke: Erotic Poems (forthcoming anthology,
    Tupelo Press): "Hypothesis, Proof"

Contents

Wherever you are, we must do the best we can. It is so far to travel and we have nothing here to travel, except watermelon sugar. I hope this works out.

RICHARD BRAUTIGAN, *In Watermelon Sugar*

I.

Point of Origin

I don't remember much. A feeling of pressure.
Then someone took the cover off.
But it wasn't happily ever after; more like the ocean,
flat and smooth until you can't stand it, then...
regrets. I get sick a lot. I was born
in Cleveland. I stuck a hairpin in an outlet.
So many ways to be disqualified.
My daughter rolls her eyes and I wonder
where she went, hope she'll come back—this,
after working furiously not to be needed.
Even so, I'm starting to like the way life
tosses you around, though it goes
against my true nature. My true nature
is to sit in the shade, watch the birds
at their business and envy them, but not enough
to think I can fly. Not enough to fly.
Once there was a girl who lost her way home;
she knocked on no one's door.
My true nature is to feel uncomfortable, worry
I've said too much. But I won't
take it back. That's why I'm still standing
here, half in the light.

If You Get Stuck

Think small. Rules, as opposed to statutes,
daisy, not hydrangea. Take one
of anything—cracker, teacup, eyelash—and look at that,

the dark c-curve of what you were going to wish
still stuck to your fingertip.
Everything's got something to say,

but for now it's the fire you're listening to
breathe in the grate.
Between its faint heat and tomorrow there's more

than just getting through. Problem is the cup
never quite fills; somewhere on that meniscus
lies a tipping point. If only

you understood science, or commitment,
how people do it: *Don't Sweat the Small Stuff.*
It would be good to have room for a sticker.

Or a t-shirt—*I'm With Stupid*, big arrow pointing up,
meaning you, or the blue-black sky
throwing its beauty around, regardless.

Lost & Found

I lost the color red: wagon, stop sign, corduroy jumper.
I lost the park when it began to thunder
and we waited out the storm
in a bunker of wet, gray wool, rubber toes
touching to protect us from lightning.
I lost the sisters who babysat when my mother
allowed herself to get desperate,
the girl on the fourth floor
who dropped her cat off the fire escape
six times before it broke a leg.
I lost the buckeye trees, two long blocks
to school, the intersection I learned to cross,
the man in the car with something on his lap
he wanted me to see. I saw.
I lost the Band-Aid colored slip
peeking out from my teacher's dress
as she read to us from Grimm's, the book fanned out
to where the thoughtless, innocent, hungry
wrens erase Hansel's breadcrumb trail.
I lost the name of the boy with dark eyes
we drove home from school, the two of us in back
elbowing, smiling. Sometimes I think
I'm still looking for him.
I lost the room I shared with my sister, narrow bed
where I looked out at the sky,
and I lost my sister. She's back, but not really.
I lost the first day of 6th grade, stepping off the bus
in my platform shoes, Meg asking me
if her paisley shirt was see-through.
I said no. That's what friends do.
I lost Soul Train, *Superstition*,
doing nothing, taking turns, doing nothing.
I lost my boyfriend teaching me
to kiss: *put your tongue here.*

I lost books I stole from my parents:
Sartre, Beckett, Eliot, *In Watermelon Sugar*,
and thought, "Well, what is this?
What am I supposed to know?" I lost paintings
I accepted without hesitation, their nudity, violence,
abstraction and the artist who said
I looked like a Picasso etching, the kind
where the women are gourd-shaped, naked, missing
one eye and I wondered how he could
see that. Did he see that?
I lost a through-line, bellwether,
gravitational pull, the point
where rays eventually intersect. I failed geometry
twice. Followed no marked path. Held on
to my radar or whatever it is
pulsing OK, OK,
you–my–sweet–twisted–up–girl–are–done.

Cake & Eat It Too

I'd hoped to be admired but would've settled
for included, hunkered as I was

on the floor with the cat cleaning her face, me
licking my empty wine glass,

but in struts Beauty, bluebirds
power-lifting garlands to bedeck her

diaphanous spring suit—ta da! Abundance
followed closely by Envy, to which I respond

with too much cake, bad behavior,
and the requisite apology: sorry

I looked so long at the mother-of-pearl buttons
on your black cowboy shirt

that what I imagined spilled out, slopping
fake fairy dust over everyone

I couldn't quite rub off. It's just I was hungry,
and the appetizers were all one kind of cheese

arranged in different shapes; kind of like
when you've been married

a long time. I've been married a long time.
My husband used to wear shirts like yours

he made himself on his mother's ancient Singer.
He won a contest in 4-H. He kicks ass

in Sudoku. These are stories about him
I love to tell. It's almost midnight. Come close.

I'll whisper them to you,
take good care of those buttons.

Hypothesis, Proof

A week of nonnegotiable fantasy, days
of unmovable image—in a locked room,

against a door, in front of the window.

I, of course, am wearing a skirt, stockings
holding onto my thighs. You look

and then look down. You think

what you think. There's only this table
between us – a slight expanse

of wood and steel, file cabinets,

note-taking. You rely on me
and I you, not to. But I'm undependable

with the right kind of pressure.

I look outside at the land you love
clearing its throat, preparation

for singing. We have an understanding.

A bridge arches over the river, river
rises to meet it, pigeons fly out

from the dark underneath, and starlings

rise and fall in parabolic sweeps, glissandos
drawn from architecture and math, music

almost impossible to play.

Dear Tender Place

above my right ankle
where they inserted the needle.
Dear sensation. Dear mole on my thigh
that isn't so sexy. Dear world
and the way things happen:
bare limbs framing paper cut
ridges, pumpkins softening
on the stoop. Dear crooked, caved-in
smiles. Dear good intentions.
Dear deer running away
from hunters high in the trees
sipping coffee as they wait
on their little wooden platforms.
Dear dead animal.
Dear ruminants that stand and stare
at the fence, horses hoping
for apples, dog angling
for a good, long walk. Dear pain
I hope isn't a neurologic disorder
inherited from my mother. Dear
mother, I miss you. Dear mother, I regret.
Dear mother, I have a daughter
who loves and dismisses me.
I made it no closer to the sun.

Of All She Surveys

The day began as failure and became a field
with the wind blowing through.

Not empty: someone's laid out a blanket,

sun, bread, sky—even the fool
dog that jumps, upsetting the wine,

and at the bottom of the field, looking so small

I almost mistake them for rabbits,
my children.

As usual, she quit the game half-way,

and he—cheated, bereft—proceeds to fall apart.
But she dangles a crown, promises

buttercup, daisy, clover

and he brightens. I'm happy here, too,
watching the sun get lost

behind milkweed clouds, listening

to his grief evaporate and her song carry,
though I catch only half on the wind.

Song I taught her and forgot. Song she weaves.

Maybe I'm queen, maybe she is.
You'd think I'd get the difference

between descent and ascent,

dissent and assent.
After so much careful looking, looking

and refusing to look,

you'd think I'd know plenty—
that snake in the grass—when I see it.

Fruit of the Loom

They came rolled in cigar-shaped bundles,
six to a pack, and somebody's hands
stuck a thin strip of clear tape
to keep them snug in their plastic
bassinet like blind newborn puppies,
(needing, no doubt, to hunker down
for their long trip) and as I stood there,
surrounded by unfresh laundry, peevishly
picking bits from each pair, I wondered
about the person, the taper, and whether they stood
or could sit, and if they got shit
for using too much tape and if they thought
of us: American women with wide hips
or boyish bottoms who buy bright bikini
underwear, the elastic emblazoned with a name
reminiscent of another era, when America
still made stuff to sell, and women who didn't
or couldn't marry or farm could work
all day in an airless room moving
cotton from one machine to the next, cotton
picked by people not far from slavery, sent north
by trains trailing smoke from coal
mined by men working in the dark with dark
in their lungs; coal, cotton, trains and mills
with girls treading the wide pine floors,
and because I'd now firmly attached the hands
to someone female, I imagined the taper
Honduran, Bangladeshi, Vietnamese, a woman
rolling, taping, packing, not yet letting herself
look ahead to finishing, and I saw again
the woman I watched in the parking lot
today, trying to stop crying, get out of the car,
pick up her kids from school.

Happy as I Believe Myself to Be

Three days I was all yes, seeing only luscious,
early summer light. For three days
grateful, pompous even, I idled
in my blowsy garden rampant
with vetch, forget-me-not, trumpet vine
springing forth from the head of a split pin oak
in crazy, vegetative fireworks. My car
sat in the driveway so long a spider
rigged a zip-line from roof rack to lilac;
not a web, just a filament
catching the breeze. *Why there?*
I asked, watching the dog puzzle out
the perfect spot to bury his bone—*here,
no here, not here, no, yes, here*—
and return dirty-nosed, triumphant,
like it was a game both of us were winning.

When I Couldn't Turn Disappointment into Something Sweet

no matter who asked me, the moon rose up, all pockmark
and pancake, throwing light on everything,

indiscriminate, as if fall and squawking katydids
could make up for a summer thick with truncated choices—

who to hurt least, how to do it quickly, stop pretending
I had a plan. No one's watching the grass grow.

No one's counting leaves as they turn, and who else notices
how each day my hands become more my mother's, more terrain

I've barely mapped? Now this road and this moon,
this wind I'm thinking could've blown in from anywhere,

could've been blowing the day my father died, through the cemetery
this same wind throwing my hair around, someone's grocery list,

plastic flowers, tears and wind in the box they buried him in,
wind in the cars we drove away, in our lungs the wind of that day,

held and released, little by little, rising up, and in the wind
grief of people I'll never meet, strangers to me

and this wind in their faces, between houses, standing
or in ruins, in dark, small places, running through the soft fur of animals,

this wind is singing in the mouths of birds, in canyons, through afternoons
of patience worn thin, scarcity, due diligence, longing, that ache

we might feel, if just for the sake of experiment, we lay naked
in a room with the windows open, testing the probability,

no matter how played out or remote, that someone might
find us and know what to do, how to touch us.

Given Flowers

Here, roses leave shadows on the ground

I hear the nodes of the rosebush
of little leaves opening stickily
the sap pushes, raising the rose

And all the daffodils
are blowing, and the bright blue squills

Let the flowers make a journey

Goodbye to the lilacs planted by the door
the lupines like apostles
cornsilk and alfalfa, drawn milk of the humdrum
one clover, and a bee

I wanted this morning to bring you a gift of roses

the rose in bloom
the rose in seed
bonfires of roses in the snow

This Paradise

Last night, late, dogs barking.
Earlier, tree frogs
announcing their way out of mud.
Now a cardinal calls for a mate,
one-note, plaintive,
so many times I get up and shut the window.
Do birds get hoarse?
Daffodils, as usual. Crocus and squill,
the lilac's closed buds, tight, like a baby's fist.
Am I done with that?
Last week a trip to the ocean;
kids searching out bits of colored glass
before they turn to sand. I was certain
I felt the tide pull.
At the hotel I caught myself
in the mirror. Brief recognition,
as if a bird flew across my eyes.
The calendar blooms.

She Continues

May I continue?
There've been several interruptions,
but let me just say that I, the Mother,
would not have let myself
at four run away to join the circus
with a pastry box
jammed full of kittens. Busy as I am,
I at least would suggest
a sturdier box.

As it was, by the time we got home
the kittens were all over
the back of the squad car. My mother
with sleep on her body
answered the knock,
the screen door held fast
against the shock, and the mama cat
scratching to get at the prodigals.

I'm sure I left cat hair in the cruiser,
fingerprints on the vinyl seat.
The cop left an imprint
on the blistering screen door, his hand
ate some of the paint away,
he digested us, my mother naked
beneath her robe, the susurrus of her
breath against the screen.
We passed through him.
We continue.

★

My daughter needs me to
continue. To move
not toward dust but seed.

All that work to get her out and now
she's desperate, it seems,
to plant herself in me. She digs in
beneath my ribs so hard

I have to tell her to stop. I'm not
always nice, but I try,
I peel her off and steady her, steer her, direct
my hand in the small of her back
even as I am unmoored, drifting, bumping
into my own non-existence, not yet
death but a foretaste.

She says to me: *Promise,*
promise you'll wait
until I go into the ground
and then go into the ground with me
and we'll come back
at the exact same time.

I don't want to think of her
in the dark earth; the rectangle
of my mother has yet to grow grass
beside my father and now
a dear friend, too, "rests" in the dirt.
But I'm a good mother. I promise:

Our bodies feed the earth,
we become flowers,
it doesn't matter
how many times we die.

★

O.K., it's a fairy tale,
but if not that, what? The air
seems clear but isn't it thick

with us, with all
we're leaving behind? Energy of desire,
heat of disappointment,
spent cells, parings and exhalations—

as it is, I've got to sweep the bathroom
twice a week, there's so much
of my hair falling. Yesterday,
beside the dark comments in the sink
I found a tiny scroll, a little wet,
tightly rolled, seal unbroken:
The best profit of the future is the past.

An artist would make a big deal out of this,
but I'm just cleaning up,
it's just another grocery list to me—
forty minutes
before my daughter steps off the bus
and what do you do with forty minutes?
Sweep. Fold laundry. Stare into space. Continue.

Turning

I don't need hawk-weed or aster
to know it's time. The clock
in my belly is over-wound, birdsong
elbowed out by crickets, finches
hoarding seed, cat gone
missing. My boy grieves, and I ache
to feed him from my hand, but he's eight.
I say, *we keep pets for practice*,
meaning to prepare him—is that
what I was doing? Was it to him
I spoke? Because I stopped, could go
no further with that dark explanation.

We Go Out

We walk out from the dry fields of childhood
into the dark storm of late summer.
A walk of innocence and awkwardness
we're not even conscious of owning.
Last dream, first idea. I mean the stuff just beyond
the glass door we put in deliberately
to separate forest from trees. So we can sleep.
So we can be alone with our velvet losses, dark
questions, the place inside testimony
that makes us ask, why?
Troublemakers. Shape shifters. Awake.
The forest is for the trees, trees are for the forest,
and somewhere maybe a fox looking hard
at a woman walking her dog, a fox
that by disposition and genetics would bite and
bite again. The hand that feeds us. Our carefully
measured portion. And whatever we are
when we lock our mouths against
what we know is our hunger.

Room to Move

Beginning with the house where a girl my daughter says is mean to her lives that I'm trying not to dislike

because she's 10

and it signifies nothing, this meanness except she's hurt, like we all are at that age, every age

and I'm too old for that

except their dog came barking out of the yard and hung there growling, and even though I called the dog by name

and the door stood open

no one came and I couldn't help thinking, yep, yours is the kind of family that lets the dog bark, that doesn't nip

anything in the bud

and then I was late for the funeral, and though I didn't love the man who died, I do love his wife, and could see

the back of her crying body

and I remembered I've done this too many times and people will do it for me, my children will bury me

and I started to feel

as if I'd run out of room in my chest, a disturbance that hasn't entirely ceased, but I had to

pick up my kids

and meet a woman who would show me houses I might like better than the house we live in now

so I asked the kids to behave

(knowing full well one could do this and one almost certainly could not)

and we looked at houses, studios, patios, fancy appliances

and the last had a meadow with drifts of ragged robin, buttercup and sedges and the wind making it all move

and I got that happiness

that occurs when there's nothing but sky over me and my daughter felt it too, and my boy, as usual

found something dangerous to climb

but it was time to touch the woman on the arm and say thanks, no, the house is too expensive

and the kids got loud

and I began to think about dinner, and who was going to make it and when we got in the car my daughter said

she wished we were rich

and I thought of a celebrity I like who got busted for crack again, one of those child stars who get famous

so fast there's no where left to go

and then I had to get back quick to the place we've filled up with us, made home.

Bow Season

Trees dropped their leaves overnight.
Like tired strippers at the end of a shift,
they stepped out of g-string

and pasties, skinny arms
reaching for a cigarette, fallen robe.
Now you see through them

to the ones behind, and behind
those to the low, suddenly flat landscape.
Clouds huddled down, dark

and the moon high, higher
than it's been all year and sharp,
a perfect alabaster paring

from the Venus de Milo's fingernail.
You catch yourself staring,
and it's been like this. Kitchen thick

with the taste of November:
tea, honey, bread. Leave the sticky spoon
on the table. Leave the flashlight.

Go out. Stones keep the sun
after it's down, so you lay along a wall
built to an unnatural clarity.

In place of mortar, small bits of flint
hold the flat stones still.
From here, you hope to watch

the moon rise, but the stars
come out first. You get dark
with what's around you, become

a shadow with the contour of an animal,
or just a pool without light.
You're trying to shake off your old

uneasy coat and it hangs there,
waiting for you to step out of it,
walk upright, stay warm.

The Bed Was Made

Start here, on the blistering front stoop:
purple trumpets of hosta in bloom, flattened
yard, milk delivered to a box by the door.
Follow the narrow walk, (frost-heaved, cracked,
unskateable), past the skinny tree (unclimbable),
and a line of bushes to catch trash blowing by.
Turn left, and left again. Through lilacs
an opening, a few rough steps down, tall
grass, sky, depth and breadth. Stand here
on a September late afternoon. A perimeter
of lit windows, neighbors, your friends' parents,
ordinary and strange: her mother ate crackers
steeped in milk, his father kept photographs
locked in a drawer, her father kept her
home as long as he could. Good
intentions, tangle of bittersweet, scent
of wild grape. No one tried to explain. Not yet.
No one said, start here, this is the beginning.

II.

Somewhere Honey from those Bees

Try to see the world's backstage
machinery, its business— *Look*,
said O'Keeffe, *look closer.*
So the man on camera
keens for his wife,
and for the flicker of a signal
he's ours, the sun shines
equally—gracing, gilding,
revealing, damning—it depends
on where you stand. Looting
or surviving? Taking or taking back?
And look at the flowers— how they open
despite everything. Maybe not as full,
or bright. Maybe not as many. One baby
held aloft, fighting for air.
When my father died the sky
cleared to perfect, creeping thyme and bees
blanketed the cemetery, honey
on its way to being made.
I thought: *how could this day be*
so beautiful? How could this day be?
Look closer. Even as the water recedes
there's nothing sweet to see here.
And so the spider's patient web,
and so the bird's broken neck,
our necessary mercy.

Scenes from the Life of the Virgin

"Andrea can get by with not a lot. She's a good woman."
RUSSELL YATES

Standing	Madonna.
Madonna	on a grassy bank, facing right,
	at a fountain,
	with a lily, a bird, an unidentified donor.
Madonna	of the family bed.
Madonna	of fish-heads, fish-wife, shrew(d).
Madonna	of SKU.
Madonna	with the angel dispensing roses,
	glue, graham crackers, wipes.
Madonna	of the play structure.
Madonna	of the tumbling after.
Madonna	with creamed crown.
Madonna	of Jack-be-quick,
	Johnny, Johnny, Johnny, whoops!
Madonna	of the accident.
Madonna	with the playing child,
	bathing child, suckling child,
	child holding his cross.
Madonna	of the one–way conversation.
Madonna	in a walled garden.
Madonna	with glue gun.
Our Lady	of Snow Days,
Our Lady	of Ear Aches,
Our Lady	of the Third Time This Week,
	have mercy:
	Noah, John, Paul, Luke, and Mary
	will not rise.
Madonna	of home school.
Madonna	of spin cycle.
Madonna	with the serpent at her feet.
Seated	Madonna (fragment).
	We all fall down.

Her Vital Statistics

on a farm
on a plantation
of a Norwegian carpenter
of an admiral
of a wealthy hatter
of Acacious, bear-keeper of the Hippodrome

into a prosperous family
into a mining family
into slavery
(parentage and place of birth unknown)

orphaned at four
betrothed at five
married at 14
widowed at 20

a timid child
a rebellious child
(her early life is obscure)

smoked a hookah pipe
dressed only in white
wore short hair and called herself "William"
declared herself daughter of Ra

nursemaid, window dresser, waitress, prostitute

at night school, while raising her daughter
without sin at the moment of her own conception
standing by the cross
commanded by voices
(little is known of her life)

tennis, swimming, shooting, fencing

ordered the deaths of 500 virgins
went to the front to deliver supplies
declined the bait of a cabinet post
merciless to opponents and jealous of rivals
eventually arrested as bankrupt

heresy, animal sacrifice, sexual relations with a spirit
(evidence is scanty and controversial)

heard of only occasionally
bored and ill
banished and deposed
(irregular, broken, tentative)

cook, laundress, nurse, scout, spy

caused more outrage
reached the Top Ten
defied and even imprisoned the Bishop

of dysentery
of cancer at the age of 34
of beriberi on the way to Shandong
apparently a beggar
burnt at the stake
by firing squad
immured in her castle
taken body and soul into heaven
fiercely energetic until her death at the age of 90

"Past A Certain Point of Magnification, All Portraits Become Landscapes"

I don't look like I have vinegar for blood.
I don't look as if I fish.
It's not clear my branches are gone.
I can't risk strawberries, so I'll ask for a lamp.
(Please dispense with any symbolism you bring to light.
It's an oil lamp. It smokes).
I must remember to hang on to the fish.
(Please dispense with any notions you have about faith.
I'm a woman. My conception is maculate.)
I must remember to hang on to the lamp
(your tired, your poor).
I must remember that fruit, all fruit, is ephemeral.
I can't risk branches. I can't risk staring.
Three painted turtles on a rock.
Hold still. Hold still.
Something is breaking.

The Pea Beneath the Mattress

I was not to ruin my hands.

I touched water in the bowl when I washed my face. I touched my face. I cut meat with a knife. I held, once, a book of days given to my mother and ran my finger across the saint's gilt halo. I liked the smell of the pages. We had no animals indoors

and they wouldn't let me ride. I fingered the gimp edging my wrists. Most often I held a needle and pushed down and through, up and through. I made gardens. A unicorn. I made a forest in the distance and beyond, a castle. I did not bite the thread.

No one asked what brought me.

My maid has told me I am fair. I was welcomed, warmed, fed but not questioned. Festooned by one of my lady's not-quite-but-almost-best dresses. She buttoned me herself. They burned everything I came in. I liked the wine. I liked the smell of him. I liked best

knowing that I was new. I felt the plush of the cushions. I was offered fruit. I was part of a dance. I didn't know the figure but it seemed simple enough: two lines of men and women that moved forward and back. Some of the men looked me in the face, closed one eye as our palms met.

From which they could tell I was quality.

And when they led me to a chamber stacked almost to the ceiling with mattresses and said I was to climb, I held my tongue. There was a ladder, and I counted. Horsehair, feather, straw—twenty overstuffed pallets. A tower.

At the top I paused, the light was dim, but I could see clearly enough that the bed was empty; a blank white space. I undid what I could and sank down. I have never slept so well.

What makes a happy ending.

If indeed there was a pea I didn't feel it, though there were bruises along my spine from the buttons I couldn't reach, and this they took for proof. I wish I could lay claim to such tenderness, such fine distinction,

imagine myself a soft, silk purse. But in truth, what I did or didn't feel had no bearing. He had decided I would stay. I know now there's no brooking that. As for my hands, ruined for what they didn't say.

She Eats Her Words

The first was *me*, then *my*,
me-oh-my. Talk about a mouthful—

so salty-sweet, so fat
with sweat and secrets. I balked,

and out came *seed*: shiny, black,
tear-shaped came seed

and *dirt*, ruby-handled *shovel*,
came *barrow*, *rake* and *hoe*.

They tasted of *patience*
(not again!) so I swallowed them

whole: *garden* with *apple*, *husband*
with *heart*. I knew

I swallowed my *heart*,
but I couldn't stop. I ate

liver complete with bile;
I counted up *ribs* to *lungs*—

and then I couldn't breathe.
I couldn't believe. I had to

take stock. What words were left?
Compulsive—ate three. *Stupid*—

stuck in my teeth. *Selfish*—
saved for later. Liar—hunkered down

with *lover. Desert*—
I left alone, but *dessert*, just

or otherwise, I couldn't resist. I ate
dish, spoon, Mary, contrary,

pumpkin where Peter could keep her.
Stuffed, alone with *drama*, it all

repeated on me. I took a *bitter pill*, O.D.'d
on *sympathy*, became *aggrieved,*

got on my *high horse*
and then, of course, had to swallow

pride. It threw me and I continue,
predictably, on *foot.*

Soul Accounting

I had not minded walls.
I had some things that I called mine.
I read my sentence steadily
from blank to blank.
I breathed enough to take the trick.
I asked no other thing.

It was a quiet way.
It would have starved a gnat.

The sky is low, the clouds are mean—
the moon upon her fluent route
the reticent volcano keeps.
Cocoon above, cocoon below—

How soft this prison is!

Perhaps you think me stooping—
a little dog that wags its tail—
my heart upon a little plate
pink, small, and punctual.

Alone and in a circumstance
I saw no way—the heavens were stitched
within my reach.
The future never spoke.
Of course I prayed.
Oh give it motion, deck it sweet…
If ever the lid gets off my head…

Over and over, like a tune.

There comes an hour when begging stops—
the clock strikes one that just struck two.
On such a night, or such a night—
today or this noon—
the life that's tied too tight escapes.

Dreams are well but waking's better.

So I pull my stockings off.
Soul, take thy risk!
Bring me the sunset in a cup—

the brain is wider than the sky.

Another Poem About Happiness

I was enjoying my usual daydream:
how sometime soon,
but not too soon,

I'm going to shine.

Now, here is the substitute yoga teacher,
reedy and sweet. She talks and talks

and I want her to shut up,
get on with it, teach me something
I already know how to do.

Last night I felt expansive.

I asked some friends if what we feel
when we chant brings us closer

to our true nature,
or if it's just illusion, another dance
away from the self.

M didn't have to think about it.
B said she couldn't tell

if the chills she felt were ecstasies
or just chills.
(B's never had an orgasm.)

I didn't say what I thought;

that I'm afraid
I have no patience for patience, that I crave
preeminence of the body, the self

emptied out.

I try to bring my mind back
to the breath, lifting
my spine, lifting my skull.

Yes, I want to keep turning things over.
Yes, I'm afraid of what I might find.

Seeing things as they are,
she says, *that's a kind of love,*
and for a moment something

lifts in me,

hand raised in a friendly way—
the flag of this day
not promised, but given.

In the Tree House

I empty the rusty teapot
of blue water, mud and leaves,
retrieve pink tea cups
from the sand box, play food
strewn through the woods.
I put cups back on their hooks,
arrange ham beside pepper,
cabbage and egg.
I would live here forever

but as I sweep
sand from the burners
on the painted toy stove,
sand my six year-old calls fire—
why can't you just leave it?—
I remember this house is hers,
and I have to give it back, leave
a little fire on the stove,
the sink, fire even on the floor.

Still Life with Mother & Child

The sun squats on the horizon, all business,
gilding the trees,

the vireo and thrush commence their tit for tat,

invisible behind the leaves.
A woman, unshowered

appears poised to record something

about this scene,
for five minutes she's sat and thought

of nothing but what she sees

then a hand shoots through the frame—
this pastoral can't hold

her son. He's got ideas

about the broom, the cat, the door, the pen, the chair,
her lap. He wriggles up,

like a tadpole with half-sprouted limbs

and out of the muck stands for a moment beatific,
but just as quickly stymied. He wants higher,

and her body's out of places to go.

But he's lucky: this time
she's not so worn through

with the implacable fact of him,

that she rushes to bargain him off
with milk, something shiny, a toy, a trick

to keep him busy, make him sleep, *please*.

Since he's allowed these few lines—little king
without mercy—she raises him up,

sings to him, until he sings back.

Coyote Tree

Yesterday there were fewer, I'm sure
the tree wasn't as full—hard to tell, the bodies
strung upside down in tight clusters, hind legs
lashed and grafted to a limb, front legs
locked in perpetual motion, noses pointing,
almost grazing the frozen ground, almost
arrow-straight, perfect. They've hung there
so many days I keep expecting something
to let go, that the next time I walk by
the bodies will have fallen to the ground
beside the soft, brown apples half-sunk in dirt.
In October they were covered with bees.
I want to push them apart; open up
space and light between their bodies
the way the man who shot them so adeptly
pruned the apple to maximize its fruit.
It's been cold; from here they don't even stink.
I didn't notice at first, how did I not
see them? Today I count six, they're in season.

Overimproved

Rosa Multiflora, a tangle of blood-red hips
cut from a cascade on the riverbank,
sends out leaf and root in the glass cell
where I put it for color and because it would keep.
In this unseasonable December we enjoy
with discontent, it sends forth a green flag,
and my husband—not picky about what grows,
except that it protect us from our neighbors'
curious interest—wants me to plant it.
Invasive! I cry, but to no effect: he enumerates
its merits, its measure of beauty and inoffensive scent,
above all, its strength. What could be bad?
But I'm not sanguine; as the descendents of Darwin's
finches haggle at the feeder I'm ready
to evict them all—rose, bittersweet, honeysuckle, grape—
with their deep tap roots and linebacker habits.
Not in my backyard, I think, surveying
our cheek-to-jowl lots, formerly hillside,
28 miles down-wind of Vermont Yankee, where spent
radioactive waste cools in aging tanks, ripe
for accident, natural or otherwise. Clean,
cheap fuel. What could be bad? Imagine:
scientists are at work spinning rope from carbon,
miles of hollow cable an elevator will ascend
to the moon. Imagine who or what
that ark might carry: our irradiated seed, supersized
livestock, fish spawning in boxes
too small to swim in—like the polar bear
at the zoo: dive, touch, turn, breathe, dive—
we watched until it hurt. No, the polar bear
can't come to the moon, or tomatoes—
forget about anything animal or vegetable
that bruises—but the cockroach is probably
there, patiently awaiting our arrival, or rather
the genetically altered versions of ourselves
which resemble us exactly and are like us
not a bit, not one hair of who we are.

Self-Portrait of Someone Who's Not Me

Did I say I'm not myself?
I meant to say since my father died.
I mean since we put him in a hole
in the ground inside a pine box with a shawl
draped over it. Because that's the way
it's done. Did I say *it*? What I meant was
that's how Jews bury their dead
so we did it even though no one sat shivah
because none of us are real Jews
in the way I think real Jews are. Did I say *real*?
I meant religious. Or I meant close.
Or at least able to say prayers for a Passover
meal. Did I say *meal*? I meant seder,
in which each dish is a symbol of something
we want to celebrate and move beyond:
bitter herbs, salt water, roasted bone.
Was there something else? Grief.
I've been trying to define it,
but all I can do is keep moving,
though most of me wants to keep very still.
I say *still* but I mean held, I need to be
held, but not by somebody. Did I say *not*?
What I mean is I need to be held
by my father and mother,
but he is underground and she asleep
in a wheelchair in a corridor by a nurses' station.
So they can keep an eye on her. So she is safe.
And that is the *best* and *only* way.
Did I say best and only? I meant to say
that's the choice we've made for her.
She doesn't seem to remember she was ever
anywhere else and I can't remember
how we traversed the arc
from my father's obstinate refusal

to his death, and from his death
to the collapse of our good intentions.
By *we* I mean the four of us
children, each eyeing the other with contempt.
Did I say *contempt*? I think it's fear,
fear the others see through the elaborate
construction we've spun, this chrysalis
from which we're unwilling to emerge.
We'll sit on the porch my father built,
and if it's evening the hummingbird
will feed at the bee balm, making that
familiar blur. We'll make our decisions,
hate each other a little less or a little
more. Did I say *or*? I meant to say *and*.

How to Build a Ruin

It should appear as if it stood forever.
Not unfinished but untended, unintended.
Not a prayer. But you could
stumble upon it and be raised up.
It might resemble yearning, something
embedded you mistook for betrayal, a leak
in the roof that keeps moving around,
engineering like blindness.
You're not meant to look ahead.
You're meant to have faith.
At some point the bird will arrive,
and if it will sing, we'll know if it sings.

One and the Same Action Seen from Various Places

1.

We set out traps: black disks with bait
ants lug back to the nest. *Destroys queen*

and her colony! the box exclaims
with yellow glee. Is it a little comic? *Honey,*

*I'm home…*or just drama,
like my son's dashboard hula-girl shimmy

that tells me he's cold. He loves the ants,
and we must stop

while he points and touches, touches
too hard and *kills them dead*. No,

no knowledge yet of *kill*, just the fact
of ants. Discovery of will, his

and theirs, and maybe he gets it
that he's bigger, carries more weight.

2.

We set out traps. I'm scrubbing
last night's pan, resenting the greasy water

and an ant
ekes up the wall with its body-sized loot.

I'm trying to respect the light in all beings
and this ant shines. It reminds me

I miss my dead parents, both of whom
I keep seeing

in various bodies: sick woman, arrogant man,
angry mother, farmer

in a brand new pick-up. And the bodies
seem to accumulate: slapped mosquitoes,

burnt moths, trapped mice, flattened squirrels—
and now the birds our house is killing.

Upstairs three men swarm over walls and ceiling
tearing out, re-erecting, the house

reaches up and birds are surprised
windows aren't more sky.

3.

We set out traps. Last night at dinner
we heard it again: a body

meeting resistance. My daughter and I
pressed our faces to the screen to see

a thrush on its back. *Is it dead?*
she yanks my arm with hope? fear?

scientific detachment?
The bird twitched, tail fanning, one wing

unfurling with da Vinci precision,
(yes, the wing

came first, but didn't he make it, make us
more than the sum of our parts?)

then the other, and the bird
righted itself, flew

back into the trees. We went back
to dinner, hungry and relieved.

(O the wing! So unlike
the plucked and sauced meal on our plates.)

4.

We set out traps. On the kitchen table
a jar of peonies, their lush, ragged petals,

and I see the face of the woman who sold them,
a pale oval with something wrong—

a red seam running through. I thought:
"white splotched with crimson"

(my favorite peony) and looked away
to her flowers, buds crawling with ants.

Because We've Landed on the Moon but Nobody Wants to Live There

Someone's got to stand at the door waving,
then busy up the empty house, clear the table, dishes,

her face. Someone's got to wash away
that smear of relief and regret,

keep the birds in check,
break a few speckled eggs, then cry

as if it were all a cruel mistake. Because the eggs
are ruined. Because we never get back

that feeling of lying in the grass, breathing in
the soft earth and the whole of summer before us.

We love celebration, the smell of fireworks,
but we work too long and forget to pick up milk.

We don't notice or agree. And it's too easy
to hit someone's hand with a ruler. And a hundred times

is too many. We need to forge a different taste,
give it a name and shape,

then send an arrow through it. So we can hold
each other. So the phoebe can re-use its nest.

So flowers can bloom. So the loyal dog
can travel half a continent and return home,

limping and proud. So conversation can be more
palatable than absence—like cotton candy—

sweet, and then nothing. Even so, it anchors us
when we think we might blow away.

Grass Whistle

What I wanted was a rose, an open mouth.
What I got was this slender blade of grass;

it can sing, or cut. Stretch it taut
between your thumbs and send your breath

there. A little breath and a little time.
What comes out the other side?

Who slips out the back door?
What did you hide beneath your mattress

you wanted nobody to see?
Hold it to the light: is it smaller

than you remember? Does it still sting?
Climb down from your tree-house

and feel how the cool earth
yields to your bare feet.

That's a kind of welcome.
Remember this when you're falling,

or falling asleep, take the dream you're given,
pull the covers up tight. Who are you

tonight? This morning I'm the one
who got away. Last night the one who couldn't

run fast enough. Most of the time
I'm the one who has to choose.

I can't. My closets are bursting, the attic's full
of what I love broken or breaking.

Tonight I'll dream of what to let go.
To get ready I'll unpack, put the books

back on their shelves,
comb dead leaves from my hair,

memorize some commandments.
I can't lay down my sword and shield,

but if I stand very still I might
hear the wind move around me.

Notes

"If You Get Stuck"— this poem was written in memory of Deborah Digges.

"Soul Accounting"—each line of this poem is a first line of an Emily Dickinson poem.

"Scenes from the Life of the Virgin"— in 2001, Andrea Yates told police that she drowned her five children in a bathtub "because she had been a bad mother who hopelessly damaged them." Noah, John, Paul, Luke, and Mary are the names of Yates' children.

"Past A Certain Point of Magnification All Portraits Become Landscapes"— this title is from scientist/photomicrographer France Bourely's, *Hidden Beauty: Microworlds Revealed.*

Given Flowers—this poem uses lines from several poems in the anthology, *A Book of Women Poets from Antiquity to Now, Selections from the World Over*, eds. Aliki & Willis Barnstone.

Her Vital Statistics—this poem is made up of biographical details from *The Northeastern Dictionary of Women's Biography*, ed. Jennifer S. Uglow.

"One and the Same Action Seen from Various Places"— this title is taken from a line in one of Leonardo da Vinci's notebooks, "…every human action shows itself in an infinite variety of situations."

AMY DRYANSKY's first book, *How I Got Lost So Close To Home*, was published by Alice James Books and individual poems have appeared in a variety of anthologies and journals. She is a Massachusetts Cultural Council Poetry Fellow and has received honors from the MacDowell Colony, Vermont Studio Center, Villa Montalvo and Bread Loaf Writers' Conference. She's also a former Associate at the Five College Women's Studies Research Center at Mt. Holyoke College, where she looked at the impact of motherhood on the work of women poets. Dryansky currently works for a regional land trust, teaches creative writing, and writes about what it's like to navigate the territory of mother/artist/poet at her blog, *Pokey Mama*.